DATE DUE			
APR 2 '68			

921
Penn   PENN, WILLIAM
        Syme, Ronald
        William Penn: founder of Penns-
        ylvania

Copy 2

WILLIAM PENN

FOUNDER OF PENNSYLVANIA

WILLIAM PENN

FOUNDER OF PENNSYLVANIA

RONALD SYME
illustrated by William Stobbs

William Morrow and Company
New York   1966

copy 2

A S A SMALL BOY, William Penn always knew when his father was due to arrive home from the sea. At such times there was much dusting and sweeping and polishing in the little family house that stood on Tower Hill in the heart of London. In the kitchen the servants became busy at roasting and baking. Gallons of home-brewed ale were waiting in the cool cellar. As the busy household well knew, Captain William Penn enjoyed good food and drink.

When the great day finally arrived, a big three-masted English warship went sailing cautiously up the River Thames. Then a ten-oared boat came flying across the river toward Tower Hill. In the stern always sat short, muscular, and clean-shaven Captain Penn himself. On these occasions he appeared most handsome in a brass-buttoned blue coat, white knee breeches, silken stockings, and black, highly varnished shoes with silver buckles.

For several weeks after these homecomings the Penn house was always an exciting place to live. There was much feasting and drinking. Mysterious strangers and distinguished gentlemen arrived at all hours of the day and night. Sometimes these visitors paused to pat the small, sturdy William on the head and fumble in their purse for a silver coin.

8

During those years the whole of England was in the grip of a bitter Civil War. Fierce battles were often fought across the green, cool English countryside.

King Charles the First, the proud, stubborn, clever but dictatorial English monarch, was determined to rule the country according to his own high-handed methods. Most of the aristocracy—the Cavaliers—supported him.

Opposed to the king were the Parliamentarians. They were the humbler people of England and sturdily opposed to the Catholic religion that Charles wished to introduce. They also distrusted the whole idea of a royal dictatorship. Kings, they declared, should rule with the consent of the people.

The war between the Cavaliers and Parliamentarians broke out in 1642, two years before William Penn was born. In 1649, when he was five years old, King Charles surrendered. His army was dispersed or dead, and he himself—after a most unfair trial—was executed in the same year. Four years later, the Parliamentarians' leading general, Oliver Cromwell, became the Lord Protector of England. He was a hard-faced, bitter, and ugly man of obstinate views and temper.

Instead of having a dictatorial king, the English people discovered to their sorrow that they had ended up with a lowly born and unpleasant dictator!

William Penn, the elder, was a shrewd man. Although he sympathized with the unfortunate Charles, a man of winning nature, he did not fancy the king's chances in the Civil War. He joined the Parliamentarians whom secretly he rather disliked. During the five years that followed he fought against the Royalist ships at sea.

It was lucky for William that his father, who had been promoted to vice admiral, had little use for the dreary Puritan religion that

Oliver Cromwell and his Roundheads (Parliamentarians) favored. There were no thin meat broths and unbuttered bread and glasses of spring water in the Penn household. They continued eating and drinking as well as ever. The Puritans were opposed to rich food and fine clothes and just about everything else that made life worth living. They succeeded in creating extremely dull conditions for themselves and all those unfortunate people who had to endure their ways.

William Penn was fourteen years old when Oliver Cromwell died. The English people secretly rejoiced. They had missed their dueling, cockfighting, card playing, and horse racing. The dictator's son, Richard Cromwell, whom everyone called Tumbledown Dick, soon proved himself a failure in the role of successor to his unlamented father. Most of the British people believed that the sooner their country had a king again, the better—or at least the happier—it would be for everyone.

King Charles the Second returned to England from exile in Holland in 1660. By that time William Penn was sixteen years old and busy learning Greek, Latin, and the difficult art of writing rather pompous English prose.

Admiral Penn was in command of one of the warships that brought the king to England. No sooner did Charles step ashore than he created the admiral a knight. Possibly the old sea captain had shown more sympathy for the Royalists than Cromwell and his gloomy chiefs ever came to hear about.

A few months later Sir William Penn was promoted to serve in the English Admiralty, where his companions were all the most illustrious men in the country.

At sixteen years of age William went to Oxford University. He was becoming a handsome and well-built young man with fine manners and a love of horses. He had plenty

of money to dress in the colorful style fashionable then in England. His elegant ways distinguished him as the son of a Cavalier, or aristocratic, family. Friends and tutors declared that a bright and successful future awaited him. Among the undergraduates at Oxford he was regarded as one of their best horsemen, pistol shots, and swordsmen.

At seventeen William began to think seriously about religious matters. The Protestant

Church of England was being reestablished throughout the country. All other religions were harshly suppressed. Those who refused to conform were either deported, fled the country, or were executed. Great numbers of Puritans emigrated to America and took up residence in one of the seven existing English colonies, which were known as Virginia, New Plymouth, Massachusetts Bay, Connecticut, Maryland, Rhode Island and Providence Plantations, and New Haven.

It seemed to young William Penn that King Charles was not keeping his promise to restore religious freedom to England. Among those who were being persecuted were the Quakers. A certain brilliant theologian named George Fox had founded this strange and obstinate sect in 1647 and called it the Society of Friends. Enemies first used the word Quakers as a term of abuse. Long after the Friends proudly adopted the name for themselves.

In matters of belief the Quakers were not very different from followers of the Church of England or Protestants. Their religious services, however, did not follow the usual pattern. Anyone in the congregation could arise to address his companions. The Quakers did not believe in baptism or the taking of oaths. They dressed very plainly and used *thee* and *thou* in their speech instead of the more usual *you*.

William Penn admired the Quakers. True, they often made a nuisance of themselves with their fiery preaching in public. On the other hand, they were a mild and modest people, who believed in practicing charity among themselves and others. He began to think it was wrong that they should be persecuted in such a merciless manner.

In 1661 William was sent over to Ireland by his father to supervise a country estate owned by Sir William Penn. The stone-built farmhouse was lonely and cheerless. The local Irish had no love for their English landlords. The wet, green countryside seemed to be always obscured by cold and drizzling rain. William, who liked warmth and good company, soon became bored with his existence.

One cold, wet evening he was sitting beside a blazing fire when a servant said to him, "There's a queer fellow named Loe in the village, sir. He's been preaching about Quaker-

ism to anyone who will listen all the day."

William recognized the name. Thomas Loe had been a brilliant Oxford student. Such a man might prove good company on this miserable evening. "Take a horse to the village," he ordered. "Ask Mr. Loe to join me at supper and spend the night here."

William and the Quaker conversed beside the fire until long after midnight. They made an oddly contrasting pair. Loe was poorly

dressed, hungry, and humble in manner. William was a wealthy young man who had never gone short of a meal in his life. But they shared the belief that religious dictatorship was bad. Both men believed that all people should be free to follow any religion they chose. Before dawn broke, Penn had almost become a convert to Quakerism.

Loe trudged off in the morning and soon afterward William returned to England.

Friends quickly noticed a difference about him. He was beginning to avoid elaborate dinner parties where great arrays of wine and food appeared in endless quantities. Every now and then he impatiently criticized the waste and extravagance that were being displayed at the glittering but corrupt court of King Charles.

Among those who noticed this change was a senior official at the Admiralty named Samuel Pepys. He was a clever and observant man, although not above having sticky fingers when handling public money! Pepys has remained famous in history for his interesting diaries. Being reasonably friendly with Sir William Penn, he was able to observe much that went on in the admiral's household.

June 5, 1661: Sir W. Penn and I went out with Sir R. Slingsby to bowls in his alley, and there had good sport. I took my flageolette (an instrument like a flute) and

played . . . in the garden, where W. Penn came out in his shirt . . . . And there we stayed talking and singing and drinking great draughts of claret, and eating botargo (sausage) and bread-and-butter till twelve at night, it being moonshine, and so to bed.

Less than a year later Pepys guessed that something was amiss in the Penn household.

March 16, 1662: Walking in the garden with Sir W. Penn. His son William is at home, not well. But all things, I fear, do not go well with them—they look discontentedly, but I know not what ails them.

The trouble was William's growing enthusiasm for the Society of Friends. If he chose to become a Quaker, all the glittering opportunities that awaited him would swiftly vanish.

The old admiral was afraid that his only son might even end up by being sent to prison.

"Make arrangements for your boy to go to France," suggested some of Sir William's friends, when he confided his troubles to them. "He'll move in gay company, pick up new ideas, and be kept a long way from those rascally Quaker acquaintances of his."

William arrived in Paris in 1662, when he was eighteen years old. He already spoke excellent French, was good-looking, and held letters of introduction to many of the most distinguished families in France. Before very long he found himself in the splendid royal court of King Louis the Fourteenth. There the gaiety and extravagance outmatched anything he had seen in the court of King Charles.

The French aristocracy made a great fuss over this handsome young man. William attended many sumptuous balls and receptions, but he never forgot the oppressed Society of

Friends. He spent much of his time wandering through the dark and lonely byways of Paris, recalling his conversation with Thomas Loe.

One evening he was accosted by a stranger who insisted on picking a quarrel. Penn had never fought a duel, but his life among the hard-living English aristocracy had accustomed him to such things. When the other man challenged him to draw his sword, he promptly did so.

In that dimly lit cobbled street William Penn proved himself an expert swordsman. Within a few minutes he had flicked the man's own sword from his hand and almost simultaneously poised to deliver the final thrust. Then he suddenly stepped back, and said, "Pick up your sword and leave me in peace. I have no wish to kill."

Some passersby had witnessed this duel. News of it soon reached the French court and increased Penn's already high popularity in illustrious circles. Fencing in those days was regarded as a most gentlemanly accomplishment.

William returned to England after two years in Paris. Sir William's hopes that his son might have forgotten about the Quakers seemed to be realized. For a time the younger Penn thought about becoming an army officer. Family friends regarded him with favor.

"Sir William Penn's son," wrote the busy Mrs. Pepys in August, 1664, "is a most fashionable person, grown to a fine gentleman."

Samuel Pepys, who admired few people except himself, was less pleased. "Sir William's son," he wrote, "has a great deal, if not too much, of the vanity of the French fashion, and affected manner of speech and bearing."

Soon after William's return to England a war broke out between England and Holland. Admiral Penn was placed in command of a

fine new warship, the *Royal Charles*. He went off to sea, and with him went William, who had given up his idea of joining the army.

This seafaring experience lasted only a couple of weeks, although in those days of highly uncomfortable ships it probably seemed much longer than it really was. Sir William decided to send his son back to England with personal, private dispatches for the king, and there he stayed.

In the following year of 1665 London was afflicted with the great plague. England was a seafaring nation, and in the ships that carried her merchandise there were also rats that carried infected fleas. Before the eighteenth century England was seldom free from any plague, but the great plague was the worst of its kind. A hundred thousand Londoners died in six months; it was a time of horror when all men fled from the once busy streets.

"What a sad time it is," wrote Pepys, "to see no boats upon the river, and grass grows all up and down Whitehall court (in the center of the city) and nobody but poor wretches in the streets."

During that summer the official persecution of many of the religious sects came temporarily to an end. But the Quakers, for some reason or other, were given no such relief. Raids upon their meetings, mass arrests, and brutal sentences of imprisonment continued to

take place. Yet, as William saw daily, the Quakers continued in brave and patient manner about the streets. They took food to those who had boarded themselves up in their houses, helped to gather up the dead, and took such medical remedies as were available to the homes of the sick. In those days there were no proper hospitals and no trained nurses. Most of the so-called doctors—who had no idea what caused the plague or how its victims should be cured—had fled from London. Only the Quakers, even though great numbers of them died or were arrested, went on providing organized relief.

Approaching winter caused the plague to lessen. Sir William Penn came home in September after winning a somewhat unsatisfactory naval battle against the Dutch. He was only forty-four years old, but the life-span in those days was very much shorter than that in modern times. He was aging fast and had decided to retire from an active career. William was now twenty-one, and the admiral decided that his son should spend more time on the family's Irish estate.

William went off to Ireland in 1666, the year in which half of London city was burned down, thereby ending the epidemic. No sooner had he landed in Ireland than a rebellion broke out. He served for a few months in a hurriedly recruited regiment and proved himself a capable officer. He was offered a regular commission and had almost decided to accept it when, by chance, he again met his old friend, the Quaker Thomas Loe. As a result of that second meeting, William Penn finally decided to join the Society of Friends. This decision was to affect American history greatly.

Samuel Pepys wrote:

December 12, 1667: At night comes Mrs. Turner to see us; and there, among other talk, she tells me that Mr. William Penn, who is lately come over from Ireland, is a Quaker again . . . and that he cares for no company.

Samuel Pepys did not know at the time that William had already served his first term of imprisonment on account of his new faith.

In September, 1667, he was attending a Quaker meeting in Ireland when a soldier noisily interrupted the proceedings. Penn, the aristocratic gentleman, was unable to put up with such rudeness. He caught the soldier by the collar and ejected him from the meeting, throwing him down a flight of wooden stairs with such force that the man burst through the closed door at the bottom.

The soldier complained to the magistrates. Penn was arrested and brought to trial. The judge, after observing his handsome dress and gentlemanly appearance, declared that a mis-

take must have been made. "It is quite plain," he declared, "that this young gentleman cannot possibly be a rascally Quaker. He is free to depart."

At that moment Penn set aside privileges given to those of good family. He told the judge that he was indeed a Quaker, defended himself in a brilliant manner, but was sentenced to six months' imprisonment.

As he entered the gates of the prison, Penn unbuckled the handsome sword that dangled by his side. Handing the weapon to a bystander, he said, "Take it. I shall never wear it again. Henceforth, I walk unarmed in an armed world."

Friends of the Penn family, from the king down, were horrified to hear that William was in prison. Strings were pulled, and the jail sentence was reduced to fourteen days.

Poor old Admiral Sir William Penn was particularly distressed about the whole matter.

He had always looked forward to his son becoming a distinguished man in any one of the great careers that he could have chosen. Instead, William had now condemned himself to a life of hardship without hope of any tangible reward.

The world of those days had little love for a sect that refused to take oaths and held that an honest man's word was just as binding as any oath. Being pacifists, the Friends were against war and refused to carry arms, but they were always eager to talk and argue at such tremendous length in defense of their religion that they usually exhausted or infuriated their critics. It was probably one of those enemies who invented the story about the Quaker who suddenly surprised a burglar in his house. "Friend," the Quaker is supposed to have said, "I would not kill thee for all the world, but thou art standing where I am about to shoot!"

One of the most irritating habits of the Quakers was their refusal to lift their hat to anyone, even the king. They declared that God alone deserved this mark of respect from man.

In December, 1669, Penn was arrested for writing and publishing an essay in defense of Quaker beliefs. He was jailed in a small stone chamber under the roof of the grim Tower of London, where he almost suffocated of heat during the summer and practically froze to death in the winter.

After serving nine months in prison, Penn was set free with family assistance. He immediately began drawing public attention to the miserable existence led by thousands of Quakers who had been imprisoned because of their religion. His untiring efforts led to many of these people being released. In 1670, when he was only twenty-six years old, Penn struck a blow in defense of national freedom that made his name famous throughout England.

He and another Quaker, a merchant named William Mead, were arrested on a charge of being "disloyal persons who committed the dangerous and seditious practice of meeting in public to contrive rebellion."

Mead was a sturdy ex-soldier, who had fought under Cromwell during the Civil War. Together they confronted the magistrates judging their case in a crowded courtroom. Both men pleaded not guilty.

While being arrested the two had lost their hats. The chief magistrate knew that Quakers insisted on wearing hats in a court of law. Hoping to trap Penn and Mead, he ordered hats to be brought and placed on their heads. No sooner had this action been taken than he ordered them to remove their hats. They refused to do so. Chuckling unpleasantly, the magistrate fined them fifty dollars each.

"I desire," said Penn quickly, "that it be observed that we came into court with our hats *off*. If they have been put on since, it was by order of the magistrates. Therefore, not we but the magistrates themselves should be fined."

The listening crowd roared approval. Angry and flustered, the magistrates ordered the people to be silent.

Penn's companion, Mead, also displayed fearlessness. A witness had *seen* Penn at the harmless prayer meeting in a public street, but had not heard him say anything. The same witness had not seen Mead there at all.

"What do you say, Mr. Mead?" inquired a magistrate. "Were you there?"

"It is a maxim of your own law," Mead replied, "that no man is bound to accuse himself."

Once again the crowd roared with pleasure. The judges angrily directed that Penn be

41

placed in the "bale-dock," "a well-like place
at the farthest end of the court in which he
could neither see nor be seen by the judges,
jury, or public."

But Penn, now in a blazing temper, used
his great strength to hoist himself up the side
of this enclosure and shouted his protest to
the jury before they withdrew to consider a
verdict.

"You are Englishmen," he cried. "Guard

your democratic rights. Do not give away your hard-earned freedom."

It was clear that Penn and Mead were not "disloyal persons," nor had they held their prayer meeting with any intention of causing a public riot. But the magistrates wrongly directed the jury to return a verdict of guilty against both men.

Penn's shouted message encouraged and inspired the jury. Scared but obstinate, they refused to return a verdict of guilty. They were again locked up and once more told to carry out their instructions. This time they were left in a bitterly cold room without fire or food. Once again they refused to bring in a verdict of guilty. Even after a whole night of cold, hunger, and thirst, they still refused.

The magistrates were unable to inflict a prison sentence on Penn and Mead and merely ordered them to pay small fines. By their courage the twelve jurymen proved to all England that, even in those days of rigged justice, a jury composed of honest Englishmen could not be forced to return an unjust verdict. The case has remained famous in British legal history until the present day.

Two years later, at the age of twenty-eight, Penn married Gulielma Springett, a Quaker girl of good family. In that same year of 1672 he began thinking about the establishment of a Quaker colony in America. First it would be

necessary to obtain an unsettled tract of land, where Quakers would be free to practice their own religion. Penn knew that in most of the American colonies Quakers and others were receiving little better treatment than they got in England.

In all the early colonies except Rhode Island, the gloomy Puritan spirit was thriving. Religious persecution existed almost everywhere. Even in more tolerant Maryland, the laws imposed branding and boring through the tongue as a penalty for certain opinions. In Virginia those who refused to attend the Established Church had to pay two hundred pounds of tobacco for the first offense, five hundred for the second, and incurred banishment for the third. A fine of five thousand pounds of tobacco was placed upon unauthorized religious meetings. Quakers and Baptists were whipped, and any shipmaster conveying them was fined.

In Boston two Quaker women, Mary Fisher

and Ann Austin, were arrested by the authorities as soon as their vessel reached port. Their books were publicly burned, they were suspected of witchcraft, semistarved in prison, and finally deported. Other Quakers reaching New England were fined, whipped, and imprisoned. Throughout New England, Quakers and all others who held unusual religious convictions were regarded as dangerous outlaws. Having left Europe to escape persecution, themselves, the Puritans in America were quite willing to set about harshly persecuting others.

"In the province that I hope to have granted to me," declared Penn to his Quaker friends, "you shall be governed by laws of your own making and live as a free, sober, and industrious people."

There was another shrewd reason in Penn's mind for hoping to obtain an unsettled tract of land. The Indians in that region would not have acquired bad habits from European settlers. The first adventurers in America almost all agreed that the Indian tribes they met were friendly and mild-mannered people. But when those same Indians were wronged by rascally settlers or plied with potent spirits to which they were not accustomed, they became vengeful and treacherous, and could never be trusted. At the time of the frightful Indian massacre in the Virginia colony in the year 1622—during which over three hundred men, women, and

children were murdered—the settlers believed they were living on perfectly friendly terms with the natives.

In 1680 Penn petitioned King Charles for a land grant. The king had become indebted to Penn's father, and he chose to pay off the debt with land instead of money. Thus Penn obtained a title to an unnamed tract of land that stretched northward from the Maryland frontier to somewhere near the Delaware

River. On the east this almost unknown territory was bordered by prosperous New Jersey, a rich and fertile state abounding in venison, fowl, fish, corn, and wheatfields.

Penn stipulated that the western boundary of this region should extend as far as that of Maryland. But so little was known of American geography in those days that the lawyers could accurately define neither the southern nor the northern boundary. Penn did not want to quibble about this tiresome matter. He had learned that the new territory was composed of the same rich soil as that of New Jersey and that the Delaware Indians were said to be unspoiled by contact with Europeans.

A charter was drawn up in 1681 with King Charles's approval. Penn was made proprietor of this splendid new province. It was decreed that he should have free and undisturbed use of harbors, rivers, soil, woods, mountains, all living things in the waters and forests, and all precious minerals and gems that might be discovered. In return he must pay the king a yearly fee of two beaver skins "to be delivered to our castle of Windsor on the first day of January in every year." One fifth of all gold and silver ore was also the king's.

Penn's idea was to christen the territory with the name New Wales or Sylvania. But a senior official at the royal court, apparently a Welshman, objected to the name of his country being given to a worthless and distant part of the world inhabited by nobody but some painted savages. He agreed that the word Sylvania, which means *woodlands,* might be used and brightly suggested that Penn should put his family name in front of it.

This idea disturbed Penn's Quaker sense of modesty. He begged King Charles that the country should be known merely as Sylvania. But Charles insisted that it should be Pennsylvania.

Penn then horrified a number of his friends by showing them some of the clauses he proposed to include in the constitution of Pennsylvania. His ideas were so far in advance of the age that many regarded him as a dangerous revolutionary and a menace to society.

Those particular clauses exist in modern American democracy and everyone takes them for granted. Penn declared that members of the Pennsylvania Assembly should be elected by secret ballot. All mature men should be eligible to vote and serve as members. There should be no imprisonment for debt. Orphan children should be educated by the state. The whole power of the state should rest with the people.

The English Quakers quickly showed much interest in this idea of emigrating to Pennsylvania. Under Penn's scheme anyone could buy a 5000-acre share or "propriety" of land for about three hundred dollars. (A sum worth many times more than it is today). For each one hundred acres the purchaser should pay him a rent—or "quitrent," as it was known—of fifteen cents a year. A poor man could rent not more than two hundred acres at one penny an acre.

To encourage wealthy emigrants to aid humble fellow Quakers, Penn offered each propriety owner fifty acres at a sum of fifty cents per year quitrent for each servant he brought over to Pennsylvania. When his term of employment ended the land was to be given free to the servant.

"In Pennsylvania we must build a proper town," declared Penn. "It shall be a place of wide streets and all the houses will stand in straight lines. We must not have dark alleys and crooked, narrow lanes such as exist in London. Each house in this city shall stand in its own grounds so that it may be planted with trees, fruit, or vegetables. Ours shall be a green country town which will never catch fire and always be wholesome."

Before the end of 1681 Pennsylvania was already being settled by numbers of Quakers, both rich and poor. By the end of that year the colony contained about a thousand people and more were continually arriving. Quietly dressed Quaker families were leaving by every ship bound for America. Sometimes these families were wealthy and surrounded by servants and great piles of luggage. Others were more humble folk whose entire worldly possessions were in a couple of stout wooden boxes and whose leather purse was nearly empty.

Penn himself sailed for America aboard a 300-ton ship named the *Welcome* in August, 1682. On the same vessel were about a hundred Quaker emigrants, all of whom were bound for Pennsylvania. Gulielma, Penn's wife, and their three children—Springett, a boy, Letitia, and William Jr., aged seven, four, and two—remained in England. Penn had recently bought a good solid house in a picturesque village. The children would live there, with plenty of servants to run the household. Mrs. Penn was not eager to endure the discomfort of a dark, damp, and smelly vessel in the storm-swept Atlantic, and even in good weather the voyage was long and dangerous—very hard on young children.

Eight weeks later the *Welcome* dropped anchor off the wooded shores of the little Dutch-built town of Newcastle at the mouth of the Delaware River. Thirty-one of the emigrants were missing. They had died of smallpox during the voyage.

Next morning the *Welcome* continued her voyage up the river to the village of Upland, which Penn renamed Chester. After transferring to a small sailing barge, he finally reached the site of the future city of Philadelphia. This place was called Coaquannock by the Indians.

It was at the junction of the Delaware and Schuylkill rivers. The wooded banks were high and bold, the adjacent land low-lying, but dry and fertile. The local clay was suitable for making bricks, and there was plenty of stone for building purposes. Penn's barge anchored in a tranquil little bay where the water was deep enough for medium-sized vessels to float in safety. On the grassy shore already stood a few scattered wood or brick houses, which had been built by the first settlers. The oldest of them—the Blue Anchor Tavern—had already stood for ten years. It was a brick-walled building, and it had served in the past as a post office, ferryhouse, and inn for lonely trappers and traders passing up and down river.

Penn himself probably invented the name Philadelphia for his city. It was composed of the two Greek words *philos* and *adelphos* meaning *love* and *brother*.

The actual site for the future town lay along

the shore of the Delaware River for about a mile and stretched back for two miles to the Schuylkill River. Vessels could reach Philadelphia by either of these navigable rivers.

"It is a lovely country," said Penn, gazing approvingly at the surrounding scene. "Let everything we build be as fair and gracious as we can make it."

Under his industrious leadership, Philadelphia began to take shape. Two fine straight streets were to run parallel to the Delaware and Schuylkill rivers and remain open to these streams on one side. These streets were connected with High Street, which was perfectly straight and one hundred feet in width. Broad street, of equal width, cut the city in two from north to south. In the center of the town an area of ten acres was reserved for the creation of a handsome public square.

A wharf was built by Samuel Carpenter, at which any ship up to 500 tons could be

River Schuykill

High Street

Broad Street

Broad Street

High Street

The Dock

N

PLAN
of the City of
PHILADELPHIA
in the Province of
PENNSYLVANIA
1683

River Delaware

moored. Wooden houses, mostly of logs, were erected with pointed roofs, balconies, and porches. In a nearby brickyard the first bricks were already being produced.

Meanwhile, the surrounding land was being cleared and the first crops planted. Where forests of oak, black walnut, cedar, cypress, and hickory had once stood, bountiful crops of wheat were already beginning to sprout. Within a year of Penn's arrival more than a

hundred brick houses had been erected and three hundred farms had been established in the nearby countryside.

Enoch Flower opened the first school before the end of 1683, for the Quakers were great believers in good, well-disciplined education. The cost of attending this school was very low. The actual terms were: "To learn to read, four shillings (sixty cents) a quarter. To write, six shillings (eighty cents). Boarding a scholar,

that is to say—food, lodging, washing, and schooling—ten pounds (twenty-eight dollars) one whole year."

A large printing press was brought over from England in 1685, to replace the smaller earlier model that had come with Penn in the *Welcome*. It was the first of its kind south of New England and north of Mexico. A busy little post office, established in 1683, gave regular service between Philadelphia, Chester, and Newcastle, and the colony of Maryland.

No one could blame Penn for being proud of this new settlement he had created from the wilderness. "I must say with vanity," he wrote, "that I have led the greatest colony into America than ever any man did on private credit. . . . With the help of God and noble friends, I will show a progress within seven years equal to her neighbors of forty years' planning."

Penn, the country-loving gentleman, preferred to live outside the town. He chose a site for the house he intended to build at a spot newly named Pennsbury. It lay some twenty-four miles north of Philadelphia, close to the green and lovely shores of the Delaware River.

The house was to be three-storied, built of red brick, and roofed with tile shingles. The front entrance faced a long, tree-lined walk that led to steps at the waterfront where the barge in which he normally traveled to Philadelphia floated conveniently at its mooring.

Before almost everything else, however, Penn set out to make friends with the Indians. He held a number of meetings with them, the greatest of which, according to legend, took place at a spot named Shackamaxon. It lay just north of Philadelphia, and a great elm tree was said to have marked the site. This tree was twenty-four feet in circumference and was estimated to have been nearly three hundred years old. It was eventually blown down in a gale in the year 1810.

The Delaware Indians were the most numerous tribe at this famous meeting, which later became known as the Great Treaty. They were tall, broad-shouldered, and narrow-waisted people, who went almost naked in summer except for moccasins and a waistcloth. During the colder months they wore a blanket or skin around the body and usually leggings as well. Their brown skin was carefully greased with bear's fat as a protection against insects. The heads of the young men were shaved except for a tuft of black hair left on the top. They ate meat and cooked vegetables and corn, and spent most of their time hunting and fishing. Although they had been defeated in battle by the fierce Iroquois warriors, who regarded them as cowardly, the Delaware Indians still bore themselves in a proud and independent manner.

The Great Treaty was the most important event in the early history of Pennsylvania. It was later described by a famous French historian as the "only treaty between Indian nations and Christians which was never broken."

Paintings of this famous scene usually depict Penn as a short, fat old man. However, the best artists do not always make the most reliable historians! Penn was only thirty-eight years old, and both tall and extremely well-built. His muscular strength was, indeed, out-

standing. A lady who was present at the meeting declared that he was "the handsomest, best-looking gentleman she had ever seen."

Penn wore a fine blue coat, white silk stockings, and brightly polished black shoes. He appeared riding a splendid brown stallion of high-spirited temper, which was greatly admired by the shrewd-eyed Indians as a horse of rare and wonderful qualities.

"I must make it my business," Penn had declared shortly after his arrival in America, "to understand the Indian language. I do not want to find myself having to use an interpreter. Only when I speak to them in their own tongue will they perhaps learn to have confidence in me."

Being a great scholar, who was already fluent in Greek, French, and Latin, Penn determined to master the Delaware language. When he rose beneath the wide branches of the elm to address the packed and silent rows of seated Indians, he spoke flawlessly in their local dialect. Even his gestures were the same as those used by the best of the Indian orators.

"I and my people," declared Penn, "never use the rifle nor trust to the sword. We meet the red man on the broad path of good faith and goodwill. We intend to do no harm and we have no fear in our hearts. We believe that our brothers of the red race are fair-minded and prepared to trust the friendship we offer."

One by one the Indians rose to reply. "Our tribe," one declared, "desires only peace with our white brothers. Let the peaceful smoke of your campfires blend with our own. If each race remembers the words that have been spoken today, our sons, grandsons, and generations yet unborn will come and go among the villages in peace and freedom."

During the months that followed Penn took the Indians at their word. He often visited their

camps, ate their food, and joined in their games with such vigor and strength that he defeated many warriors who were younger than himself. The day came when an Indian could pay a white man no higher compliment than to say to him, "You are like our friend William Penn."

Penn's first visit to America lasted only two years. His decision to return to England was the greatest mistake he ever made. As long as he remained in Pennsylvania, the obstinate, contentious, and stubborn people were prepared to recognize him as the outstanding leader among them. As soon as he departed, other would-be leaders were soon to arise. They would bring little except argument and doubt to the growing colony.

Penn reached England in October, 1684. Four months later King Charles, who had proved a good friend to him, died unexpectedly. With the passing of this king, dark times were soon to visit Penn.

James the Second, who then came to the English throne, was a foolish and incompetent man. During the three short years for which he reigned before being kicked out, muddle and confusion spread throughout the country. Persecution of the Quakers, which Charles the Second had managed to restrain to some extent, became more brutal. While Penn was fighting for the hundreds of Quaker families who soon found themselves in prison, news reached him that Lord Baltimore, the governor of Maryland, was angrily disputing the boundary line between Pennsylvania and Maryland. As if these fresh troubles were not enough, the Pennsylvania Quakers began to be difficult about paying their quitrents to Penn. Philadelphia was now becoming a prosperous young town of 671 houses and held a population of 4000.

"I am sorry for your squabbles," Penn wrote to a trusted friend in Philadelphia. "For the love of God, me, and the poor country, be not so noisy and open in your quarrels."

To his lawyer in Pennsylvania Penn wrote in 1687, "I am forced to pay bills here for the support of my family. I have owing to me four or five hundred pounds per annum in quitrents but . . . I have not had the present of a skin or a pound of tobacco since I returned to this country."

The Quakers were being utterly greedy and ungrateful. Their colony was flourishing. Many wealthy merchants had set up in business, opened well-stocked shops, and launched several well-built ships. Near Philadelphia there were plentiful young orchards and wide acres of cultivated land. But while Pennsylvania flourished, and every year more and more fertile acres were being acquired from the friendly Indians in the Susquehanna Valley, the sour-faced, black-coated Quaker settlers considered that money sent overseas to Penn was wasted. Selfishly they forgot it was Penn who had brought them to this country in the first place. They left him to endure semipoverty while they built new brick homes for themselves. To avoid payment of quitrents, they even began to make false complaints against Penn and his chief officers.

In 1699 King James fled from England. To the throne came a moody, silent, but capable

Dutchman named William. He was the nephew of King Charles, but regarded Quakers with a vague dislike and suspicion.

Penn soon found himself without friends or influence in royal circles. In February, 1689, he was arrested "upon suspicion of high treason," and again imprisoned in the Tower of London. This time he was detained for less than two weeks. A great many influential people still recalled how the Penns had helped the earlier kings, and how William Penn himself had defended British justice in the "bale-dock." In any case, the charges laid against him were proved completely false.

"If I could sail tomorrow for America, I would be a happier man," said Penn after his release. "How unfortunate it is that the fine tree I have planted in that country has its roots here in England. Unless one tends them carefully, the whole tree might wither and die."

Meanwhile, the Quakers in Pennsylvania

were still squabbling among themselves like a pack of overgrown children in the absence of their teacher. King William finally came to the conclusion that the only man to govern these tiresome, talkative, and tedious people was Penn himself. He merely insisted that the colony should contribute eighty men for its defense in the event of war and pay $5000 a year into the colonies' war fund. It was a perfectly fair request. France and her Indian allies

were becoming more powerful yearly and threatening the colonies.

In 1694 Gulielma Penn died at the age of fifty. She left three children, of whom Springett was nineteen, Letitia fifteen, and young William, who was becoming a troublesome boy, just fourteen. This personal loss caused Penn to delay his intended return to America, probably on account of his children.

In 1696, when he was fifty-two, Penn married thirty-two-year-old Hannah Callowhill. She was a quiet, capable, and sensible Quaker woman, who at least managed to make William, the younger son, behave himself at home. In that same year, Penn wrote, "I am a crucified man between injustice and ingratitude in America, and extortion and oppression here in England."

He had plenty of reason for complaint. Up till 1688 he had lost $70,000. By 1696 his total losses had increased to $147,000. Not being a shrewd businessman he had failed to realize that his trusted secretary, a rogue named Philip Ford, was swindling him left and right.

Penn sailed again for America in the year 1699, fifteen years after his return from that country. He spent three months crossing the Atlantic Ocean and landed with his family at Chester on the Delaware River on the first day of December.

Great excitement had arisen throughout

Pennsylvania when it became known that he was returning. He had been absent so long that his name was thought almost to be legendary. The banks of the Delaware River were lined with great crowds of trappers, farmers, hunters, Indians, and bonneted women.

Philadelphia, which now had a population of 6000, had become, after Boston, the second largest city in the New World. Seven hundred dignified houses faced the wide, tree-lined

streets. Mostly they were built of brick and ornamented with graceful porches and balconies and spacious windows. Every house stood in its own grounds, just as Penn had planned. These homes were surrounded by fruit trees and well-kept gardens. Big seagoing ships were handling cargoes of maize, wheat, whale oil, lumber, and furs. Whichever way he glanced, Penn saw prosperous streets, handsome schools, and flourishing warehouses or shops.

His house at Pennsbury had been neglected during his long absence in England. While workmen were busy putting it in order again, Penn and his family stayed in Philadelphia for the winter. In the early spring they proceeded to their new home.

The house was both roomy and handsome. The beds were draped in satin and quality linen. The furniture was largely oak and walnut. Broad oaken shelves round the big entrance hall were adorned with gaily patterned dishes and highly polished pewter mugs.

Hannah's child, John, the first of five, was born at Pennsbury the following autumn. By that time Penn was hard at work trying to restore peace among the various factions that were causing trouble throughout the colony. Those narrow-minded Quakers of Pennsylvania deserved the description of them given by an enemy, "As cantankerous a lot of folk as ever reached America."

Penn himself, in spite of his wonderful patience, once remarked, "I wish that our people would be as quiet and amiable and as honest in their intentions as the Delaware Indians."

In the Legislative Assembly of Pennsylvania there was endless squabbling. But in the tents and villages of the Indians Penn found only peace and friendship. The Delawares had never forgotten him. Being fifty-five years old, he was no longer able to wrestle with the young warriors or defeat them in grueling footraces. Instead, he went hunting with them and made a reputation for himself by the practiced ease with which he shot running deer or wild turkeys on the wing. It was not surprising that as time went on, Penn spent more and more of his leisure in the peaceful atmosphere of his home or in the smoky, but lively camps of the Indians.

He was leading a life that suited him. He looked forward to spending the rest of his

days in the wide and beautiful countryside that surrounded Pennsbury. England held only bitter memories for him. In America he had servants, horses, and acres of fertile soil that brought forth profitable crops.

But misfortune again overtook him. In 1701 he heard that the British government was considering the annexation of Pennsylvania and placing the colony under a governor sent out from England. Virginia, New Hampshire, Maryland, New York, and Massachusetts had already become royal colonies. Determined to preserve Pennsylvania as a free colony, Penn returned to England once again.

Wistfully he said good-bye to his comfortable home, the great forests he loved, the quiet-flowing river, and his friends both European and Indian. "God willing I shall return," he said. "I only wish that I were twenty years younger and no Englishman. Then I might be free to enjoy the rewards of my labors and

receive some return for all the experience I have gained."

Penn sailed in November, 1701. He wanted his family to remain in America and enjoy greater comfort than they would ever find in England, but his wife insisted on accompanying him.

"Penn had plenty of land under cultivation," wrote one of his friends. "The fields gave him corn and meat, the rivers abounded with fish, and the air gave him stores of birds for his table. To live in America with little or no money was easy enough, but to remove his family across the Atlantic was an expensive affair."

The sad thing was that he could just as well have remained in America. In March, 1702, King William fell from his horse and was killed. The British government abandoned the idea of taking over Pennsylvania. But by that time Penn's financial affairs were in such a

muddle that it was impossible for him to return to America.

In 1704 his son William made a one-year visit to Pennsylvania. He was no Quaker; indeed, he was already a wastrel and drunkard. The sturdy settlers had no use for him. They slapped him into jail for threatening conduct with firearms, told him to behave himself in the future, and nicknamed him William the Waster.

Penn's last years were brightened by two events. First, he was restored to royal favor. Queen Anne, who followed King William, was the daughter of James the Second. During her reign persecution of Quakers in England ceased. Second, the rogue Philip Ford died in 1702. His false claims against Penn for enormous sums of money were heavily reduced by a judge in court. Even so, the aging Penn was a ruined man.

"O Pennsylvania! What hast thou cost me?" he wrote. "About thirty thousand pounds more than I ever got by it. Two dangerous and most fatiguing voyages, troubles and poverty here, and my child's (William's) soul almost...." Penn was overcome by sudden illness as he wrote these words. He never made a full recovery.

One further success brought pleasure to him shortly before his death. The people of Pennsylvania suddenly realized how badly they had treated him and made an honest effort to put matters right. In 1710 they held an election that threw out all the troublesome old members of their Legislative Assembly. The newly elected members were men who had always shown friendship toward Penn, and they brought joy to Penn's heart by prohibiting the importation of Negro slaves into Pennsylvania.

Seventy-six-year-old Penn died on July 30, 1718. So ended the life of a great man who had always remained unafraid of judges and critics, spoken fearlessly to kings, and created a prosperous settlement in the heart of the American wilderness.

Penn's wife, Hannah, saved Pennsylvania for the Penn family, and the colony remained under a Penn government until the American Revolution. This quiet, capable woman managed the family finances in England and made her five children rich in later years. Until

1727 she also managed her late husband's interests in Pennsylvania, although during the last few years of her life she was a semi-invalid.

Of her four sons, it was Thomas whom she chose to take over William Penn's responsibilities in America. Thomas Penn landed in Pennsylvania in 1732 when he was thirty years old and had already received a sound business training. Before very long the settlers realized that Thomas was determined to insist on his rights, including the payment of quitrents. The rents were soon being punctually paid, otherwise the landholders were flung off their farms.

When Hannah Penn died in 1727 at the age of fifty-seven she knew that Pennsylvania had been saved for her sons. And for nearly fifty years after her death, to his own death in 1775, the shrewd, outspoken Thomas remained the real ruler of Pennsylvania.

BIBLIOGRAPHY

Braithwaite, William Charles, *Beginnings of Quakerism*. New York: The Macmillan Company, 1932.

Carter, E. H., and Mears, R. A. F., *A History of Britain 1485-1688*. Oxford, England: Clarendon Press, 1952.

Grant, Colquhoun (Mrs.), *Quaker and Courtier*. New York: E. P. Dutton and Company, 1907.

Peare, Catherine Owens, *William Penn*. London: Dennis Dobson, 1956.

Pepys, Samuel, *Diary and Correspondence of Samuel Pepys*. Notes by Richard, Lord Braybrooke. New York: E. P. Dutton and Company, 1924.

Pound, Arthur, *The Penns of Pennsylvania and England*. New York: The Macmillan Company, 1932.